In this series –

The Essential Rumi Readings
Rumi Readings for Achievement
Rumi Readings for Addiction
Rumi Readings for Careers & Work
Rumi Readings for College
Rumi Readings for Communication
Rumi Readings for Family
Rumi Readings for Grieving
Rumi Readings for Life
Rumi Readings for Love
Rumi Readings for Meditation
Rumi Readings for Mental Health
Rumi Readings for Mindfulness
Rumi Readings for Responsibility
Rumi Readings for Self-Esteem
Rumi Readings for Self-Healing
Rumi Readings for Sorrow & Joy
Rumi Readings for Youth

RUMI READINGS
FOR
RESPONSIBILITY

RUMI READINGS
FOR
RESPONSIBILITY

JALALUDDIN RUMI

The Scheherazade Foundation

The Scheherazade Foundation CIC
85 Great Portland Street
London
W1W 7LT
United Kingdom
www.SF.Charity
info@SF.Charity

First published by The Scheherazade Foundation CIC, 2025

RUMI READINGS FOR RESPONSIBILITY

© The Scheherazade Foundation

A CIP catalogue record for this title is available from the British Library.

ISBN 978-1-915311-78-8

Introduction

Jalaluddin Rumi was born in Balkh, Afghanistan, in the year 1207, and died in Konya, Turkey, in 1273.

During the sixty-six years spanning this pair of dates, he produced a range of extraordinary work in Persian which, today, is classed as 'Sufi Mysticism'.

In the seven and a half centuries since his death, Rumi's corpus, which includes *The Masnavi* and *Fihi Ma Fihi*, has been circulated widely across the Near East, the Arab world, and Central Asia.

Generations of students continue to commit selections of the 60,000 verses to heart, and allow Rumi's way of thought to permeate through all areas of their lives.

Although Orientalists venturing eastward from Europe in the 1700s occasionally made note of Sufi Mysticism, they tended to witness it through the more theatrical frills – such as 'whirling dervishes' – rather than through a deep appreciation of the texts.

It wasn't until the close of the nineteenth century that the first wholescale translations of Rumi's written work began to appear in Europe.

Even then, they remained very much the purview of a few academics, whose translations were – even for the time – laden with indescribably floral and cumbersome prose.

Although in the Occident, students would find themselves scrutinizing Rumi's corpus, it wasn't until more recently that accessible appreciations of his work became available.

A few years before his death, I asked my father – the Sufi scholar and thinker Idries Shah – for his thoughts on Rumi's legacy in the West.

Sitting in his favourite chair, a porcelain cup of green tea in hand, he looked at me hard.

'I never cease to be amazed,' he said.

'Amazed by what?'

'By the way people don't take what's perfectly packaged, and ready and waiting for them, but rather obsess with something else.'

'With what?'

'With endless and nonsensical trimmings, trappings, and paraphernalia.'

My father sipped his tea.

After a moment of silent thought, he continued:

'Read Rumi in the original Persian,' he said, 'and so delicate are the verses that you have tears rolling down your cheeks. Yet here in the West, it's served up as something submerged in a thick, glutinous gravy, so much so that its utterly inedible.'

I reminded my father that a series of publications had recently found their way to press – publications that presented Rumi's couplets in an utterly new way.

Stripped bare of what my father had referred to as 'gravy', they were light.

Indeed, they were lighter than light.

My father rolled his eyes at the thought.

'In any other place, and at any other time,' he said, 'people would be up in arms. Or, if they weren't, they'd be laughing until their sides split. Imagine it – Western poets with absolutely no knowledge of the original Persian text touting new, bestselling editions of Rumi's work! It's what we call "The Soup of the Soup of the Soup".'

In the years since my father's death, Occidental society has been flooded with all things Rumi.

Couplets ascribed to him are read solemnly at weddings across the United States, Europe, and beyond.

Wisdom drawn from his poetry is tattooed daily over the backs and limbs of Hollywood A-listers.

But the precious words uttered at weddings, tattooed into skin, and quoted in abundance, hold little or no bearing to the original verses of Jalaluddin Rumi.

So, there it is…

The great Sufi Master's wisdom available:

(a) in a form that's unreadable because it's all covered in glutinous gravy, or

(b) in another form that's completely distorted – the Soup of the Soup of the Soup.

One thing that *is* evident is that the West can benefit enormously from a clean, clear rendition of Rumi's thinking – as the East has done over the last seven hundred years.

For this reason, we have commissioned entirely new translations, gleaned in particular from *The Masnavi*. Selected and translated by native Persian-speaking scholars, the emphasis has been on maintaining the lightness of Rumi's poetry.

In an age of relentless speed and digital overload, and so as to allow the work to be accessed by those who may benefit from it most, we have arranged a series of bite-sized morsels by way of theme.

We encourage you to do what students, scholars, and ordinary people have done across the East for centuries...

To pick a single couplet, or a handful – and to read them over and over, allowing them to seed themselves in your mind.

Little by little, having taken root, they will blossom and bear fruit.

Tahir Shah

How to Use This Book

Rumi Readings for Responsibility

This is a book about choice.

About consequence.

About the quiet force within you that is always shaping the life you live.

It is not a list of obligations.

It is not a moral code.

It is a mirror – held up with gentleness and honesty.

Rumi Readings for Responsibility brings together one hundred quotes drawn from the original Persian writings of Jalaluddin Rumi, translated faithfully and clearly by The Scheherazade Foundation. These quotes are largely selected from *The Masnavi* – a work long regarded not just as mystical poetry, but as a guide to conscious living.

Responsibility, in Rumi's vision, is not just about duty.

It is about self-awareness.

It is about seeing clearly where your power lies – and where it doesn't.

It is about remembering that what you do, say, choose, and avoid – all shape the soul.

This book does not ask for perfection.
It asks for presence.

A Book for Returning To

Responsibility is not a one-time act. It is a practice.

This book is designed to be returned to again and again – as a guide, a companion, a challenge, a comfort. You may read one quote each morning, or open it at random when you feel unsure, heavy, or called to reflect.

Let it interrupt your habitual reactions.
Let it offer a pause before the decision.
Let it deepen your awareness of the moment you are in.

The quotes are arranged in ten themed parts – exploring inner and outer responsibility, leadership, consequence, destiny, community, discipline, and the soul's place in the unfolding of life.

You can read them in order, or let your need direct you. Both are valid.

Read Slowly, Listen Carefully

This book is not fast food.
It is something to be digested slowly.

After reading a quote, sit with it. Breathe with it. Let it unsettle or affirm or stretch you.

You might ask:

- What is this pointing to in my life?
- Where am I resisting what I already know I must do?
- Where have I been taking on what isn't mine?

You may not have answers right away. That's fine.

Let the question itself be part of the transformation.

Journal, Reflect, Respond

Some quotes may stay with you. Some may bring discomfort. Some may lift you unexpectedly.

You may want to keep a notebook nearby – to track your thoughts, your resistance, your growing clarity.

It's not required, but can serve as a private space to explore patterns and intentions.

Shared Reflections

Responsibility is not only a personal journey. It has social dimensions.

You may wish to share these quotes with others – in a classroom, a mentoring relationship, a leadership setting, or with someone you're accountable to.

Let them open conversations that are hard to start.
Let them offer a shared vocabulary when emotions run high.

Some of the most powerful changes come not from advice – but from a single line that shifts how we see ourselves.

Challenge With Compassion

Not every quote in this book will feel soothing.
Some are sharp. Some are direct. Some may feel like they're calling you out.

That is their gift.

But Rumi never uses shame. He uses insight. He invites you not to collapse under the weight of your missteps – but to learn from them. To choose again. To rise in a different way.

Responsibility, for Rumi, is not heaviness. It is clarity. It is power aligned with truth.

Remember: You Are Not Alone

Rumi writes in this volume:
'The remorse you feel for your misdeeds reveals that you acted by your own volition.'

In other words, the very fact that you care – that you feel, that you notice, that you regret – means that something sacred is alive in you.

Let this book keep that alive.
Let it remind you that responsibility is not just about doing more. It's about doing what's right, what's real, and what only you can do.

Return to it as often as needed.

Let it walk with you – firmly, compassionately, honestly – as you shape the life that is yours to live.

Part 1
Signs of Responsibility

1

Free will is undeniably granted to us;
this truth is self-evident,
as no one can deny what the senses confirm.
Authority, restriction, anger, dignity, and admonition,
apply solely to those given choice.
The whole world acknowledges the presence of free will,
as the command is clear:
'Do this, not that.'

2

Free will exists within us,
becoming most evident when we face two choices.
Teachers may reprimand students,
but no amount of discipline can change a stone.

3

The devil declares:
'O prisoner of body and soul,
I offered it to you,
yet I did not force your hand.'
The angel cautions:
'I warned you that your joy would lead to deeper sorrow.'
You embraced it and forsook what was rightfully ours,
failing to recognize the truth of our service.

4

The Qur'an contains many commands and prohibitions,
but who has ever given instructions to marble,
saying 'Do this or that,' when it is inert and powerless?
How could the Creator of the stars and heavens issue
commands in vain or out of ignorance?

5

The thought, 'Should I do this or that tomorrow?'
is proof of your autonomy.
The regret you feel for past misdeeds
shows that your actions were the result of choice.
If free will did not exist,
what would be the cause of shame?
What gives rise to remorse, guilt, or blame?

6

You chose a vocation for yourself, declaring,
'I have the autonomy and reason to decide.'
If this were not the case,
how would you have selected that profession
from among all the alternatives,
O master of your own path?

7

Free will is the essence of worship;
without it, the cosmos would revolve aimlessly.
Their actions yield neither praise nor condemnation,
for free will is the criterion when evaluation occurs.

8

The hand that shakes due to a tremor,
and the hand you grasp, quaking in its place –
both motions are manifestations of the Divine,
yet you cannot equate the one with the other.

9

The anger you harbour is evidence of free will;
so you cannot claim coercion
or provide a 'justification' for it.

10

The remorse you feel for your misdeeds
reveals that you acted by your own volition.

Part 2

The Evasion
of Responsibility

11

Despite clarity, the consumer, driven by greed,
ignores the light in their pursuit of sustenance.
When their only aim is to partake of bread,
they choose darkness, for daylight is absent.
If greed can obscure the sun,
how strange it is that one would disregard reason.

12

Those who persist in laziness,
lacking gratitude and patience,
are aware that they will eventually succumb to coercion.

13

The entire world, in a state of intoxication,
avoids awareness of its own existence and choices.
They surrender consciousness,
and, under the veil of alcohol and fleeting melodies,
are enveloped by inconsequence.

14

When the master handed the servant a spade,
his intention was clear without a word.
The hand, like a spade, signifies his directives;
contemplation ultimately encompasses his essence.
Gratitude strengthens you,
while ingratitude diminishes your blessings.

15

When the monarch summons you from the threshold
only to return you to that same threshold,
it is clear you have erred,
and, through ignorance, drawn coercion upon yourself.
My sustenance and fate are predetermined,
so why did that fortune slip from your grasp?

16

Why, in matters of faith,
O sceptic,
does this fear of loss cling to you?
Have you not seen how the indolent in our midst
gain advantage from the prophets and saints?

17

This restlessness, O Majid,[1]
originated from You;
otherwise, this sea would remain calm.
You have placed this turbulence within me;
now, by Your grace, free me from it.
You challenge me –
O plea for help, O man.
Why are your struggles like those of the timid?
Remove these impurities from me
so I may glimpse the garden of the virtuous.

---

1 'Majid' – one of the 99 names of God in Islamic tradition.

18

It is said that where there is smoke, there is fire, not light;
the glow of a candle without the candle is true illumination.
Yet even in the presence of unmistakable flames,
he denies their existence, clinging to his own rejection.

19

Do not contend with fate,
O swift and bold one,
for fate may turn against you.
You must submit to the decree of Truth
to avoid wounds from the Lord of the Dawn.

20

Except for the part that transcends this realm,
no appearance has been revealed through
mere pursuit or effort.
All have strayed from planning and labour;
only the actions and decrees of the Creator endure.

Part 3
Social Responsibilities

21

We do not focus on speech or language;
we examine the inner Self and the essence of existence.

22

Love and compassion are qualities of humanity, while anger and desire are the traits of animals.

23

In moments of despair brought on by solitude,
the presence of a companion
can transform you into a radiant sun.

24

Generosity views all things as reciprocation,
and recognizing this reciprocation alleviates fear.
Miserliness fails to see outcomes,
but the pearl diver delights in uncovering the pearl.

25

What is the reward for benevolence, my son?
Compassion, grace, and great advantage.

26

Refrain from dwelling among others;
focus on your own endeavours
and avoid engaging in the pursuits of outsiders.
Who is the unfamiliar individual?
Your worldly form,
for it is the source of your anguish.

27

He compromises with the opponent,
creating space for himself in their affections.
Bad habits take root through weak foundations;
the ant of desire has transformed into a serpent
through the act of repetition.
Eliminate the serpent of desire at its birth,
or it will grow into a dragon.

28

In worldly matters,
optimal conditions are maintained through balance;
the body's humours thrive through moderation.
If one particular humour exceeds its threshold
a malady will emerge.

29

Transcend the name and examine the attributes
so that your qualities may guide you to the essence.
Discord among people arises from labels;
when they focus on meaning, peace follows.

30

If God has given you an unappealing appearance,
do not also cultivate an unpleasant character.
You harbour envy, thinking, 'I am inferior to others.'
Yet this only exacerbates your shortcomings
in the realm of destiny.
Envy is a flaw and a significant defect;
it is, in fact, worse than all other shortcomings.

Part 4
Leaders & Responsibility

31

The essence of kings is derived from their subjects,
just as a fresh sky nurtures the earth.

32

O fish, see the conclusion, not the bait;
greed obscures your vision of the ultimate outcome.

33

From this ambush, no one escapes impatience and haste; patience itself serves as the tool and method for foresight.

34

How many scholars are there in the pursuit of reason?
How vast is this ocean of intellect?

35

The wise savour the world's blessings, free from sorrow;
the uninformed remain deprived within emptiness.

36

You perceived the world through a blue lens,
which is why your surroundings appeared blue.
Acknowledge this blueness as your own blindness;
criticize yourself, not others.

37

Do not let worries about sustenance burden your heart;
happiness will elude you
if you do not remain at the threshold.

38

This world resembles a delicate tree:
when it matures, its fruits become pleasing to the palate.
Unripe fruits cling firmly to the branches,
while we are like partially ripened fruits upon them.

39

O marvel, where is the oppressor in our time?
In which places is he neither imprisoned nor shackled?
When we were born, tyranny was eradicated;
so, in our day, let no oppression endure.

40

If you possess sight, do not act thoughtlessly;
    if you lack insight, adhere to a guide.
Hold the staff of wisdom and logic;
    if you lack vision, seek the staff.

Part 5

The Impact of God's Will on Human Responsibility

41

This exemplifies the influence of fate and destiny:
'You perceive the well but cannot avoid it.'
With eyes and ears wide open,
the trap lies ahead,
yet it propels itself toward the snare
with its own wings.

42

The sequence of fate and hidden mandates
which only the virtuous spirit can discern.
Though it remains invisible,
it is a concealed treasure,
more powerful than confinement and steel shackles.

43

The lion exhibits no shame regarding its restraint,
nor do we express discontent with divine will.
Despite the lion wearing a chain around its neck,
it dominates all who forge chains.

44

Begin earnest supplication.
Raise your voice in mourning, adoration, and fasting.
Proclaim: 'O All-Knower of the Unseen,
do not subjugate us beneath the weight of evil plans.'

45

If destiny envelops you in a darkness like night,
that same destiny will ultimately raise you up.
Although fate may target your life many times,
it will also grant you life and recovery.

46

Those who confront destiny will die,
succumbing to their own blood.
When the earth contends with the sky,
it becomes desolate and perishes.

47

When destiny manifests, only flesh is visible;
you cannot differentiate enemies from allies.

48

When destiny intervenes, even the doctor appears a fool,
and treatments may prove ineffective.

49

When destiny approaches, this realm begins to constrict;
even delights transform into sources of anguish.
It is said:
'When destiny approaches, it becomes limited;
vision is obscured upon the arrival of fate.'

50

When destiny manifests, wisdom sleeps;
the moon goes dark and the sun is overshadowed.
This is not unusual;
those who reject fate are, in fact, part of it.

Part 6

Responsibilities of Humans Towards God & Themselves

51

You have been called to bear witness,
to testify and resist insubordination.
O martyr, when will you extricate yourself
from this passage?
Whether in a century or a mere moment,
you must release this trust and liberate it.

52

When you express gratitude,
He will grant you sustenance free from
danger and adversaries.
Give thanks for the blessing that has set you free,
and remember the abundance of the Divine.

53

Hundreds of thousands
of chapters expound on knowledge,
yet that person remains oblivious to their own essence.
Though I know what is allowed and what is not,
do you not see whether you are truly honorable,
or merely an illusion, like a fading figure?

54

Each thorn embodies your negativity,
piercing you with every step you take.
Listen, O traveller!
The hour grows late.
The sun of your existence has sunk into shadow.
Do not say 'tomorrow', for it has already passed.
Act now, before the days of your life slip away.

55

If fate imposes suffering upon us,
how can a kind character or gentle temperament avoid it?
When will I rise from a beggar to a prince?
How can I retain my essence
if my garments grow worn and old?

56

What endeavour have you undertaken
that proved unfruitful?
What actions have you undertaken that yielded no results?
Your deeds, born of your spirit and body,
will follow you like a child.

57

Admit your faults without hesitation!
So the teacher will not claim your work as their own.
Say: 'I am unknowing; teach me.'
For self-awareness nurtures fairness.

58

Do not use fate as an excuse, young soul!
Why cast your faults upon others?
Look within to see where you have erred;
light creates movement,
while shadows merely reflect.

59

He said:

'If God wills, I shall believe;
if His grace increases, I shall attain certainty.'
Yet the Self and the devil sought to fulfil their ambitions,
causing grace to become inflamed, oppressed,
and subdued.

60

Regardless of whether the outcome is positive or negative,
your feelings of unease or elation come from within.
If you are pricked by thorns,
you have inflicted that pain upon yourself;
if you create with silk and delicate threads,
the outcome is also your responsibility.

Part 7

Humanity & the Rectification of Negligence

61

Blame yourself, O youth;
do not attribute fault to rightful consequence.
Do not be misled by the enticement of the Self,
for the sun of truth reveals even the smallest particle.

62

Repentance devoid of Your guidance,
O exalted light –
what is it but a travesty of genuine repentance?

63

If the fervour of your essence causes anguish,
allow the inferno to arise from
the decree of the sovereign of faith.
In times of sadness, pursue forgiveness;
sorrow is a manifestation of the Creator's intent –
respond appropriately, then.
When He desires, the nature of sadness
can transform into joy,
and the very constraints on your feet
can evolve into liberation.

64

Abandon strength and embrace supplication;
mercy responds to the plea of the destitute,
O impoverished one.
The plea of the desperate yearns for meaning;
the lament of the misled is merely an affectation.

65

Wherever pain exists, the remedy is directed;
wherever a boat is present, water converges.
You must show humility to receive the waters of mercy;
and therein, become enraptured by the elixir of grace.

66

O you who seek atonement for the past,
when will you atone for this same atonement?
Articulate!

67

If you have tarnished the record of your life,
repent for your earlier actions.
If time has elapsed, grant forgiveness;
this moment is your sole possession.
Water your remorse if it is dry and devoid of moisture.

68

Your transgressions have been transformed by God, turning all your past actions into acts of compliance.

69

Failure to observe the subtle intricacies of divine law
will lead to the disintegration of
every person's bodily existence.

70

Repent earnestly and pursue the righteous path,
for anyone who performs an atom's weight of good
will witness its effects.

Part 8

Human Responsibility
in the Face of God's Will

71

What is needed is surrender, not endless striving;
there is no gain in wandering aimlessly through illusion.

72

Do not let pride deceive you;
give up the grandeur of the sun and
become a mere particle.

73

Endure the divine trial
until I sever your throat as I did Ishmael's;
I will decapitate you,
yet this is a head that, in death, finds liberation.

74

The lock is strong, and the key belongs to the Divine.
Extend your hand in a gesture of submission
and acceptance.
Although many keys may be assembled, piece by piece,
only God holds the power to unlock the door.

75

I cherish Your creation,

expressing gratitude and patience.

How could I love the created while venerating the Creator?

One who admires God's handiwork is loved.

But one who reveres creation alone is misguided.

76

Why does he plead,
'O God, spare me from this decree'?
For him, the passing of himself or his children
is as effortless as honey sliding down the throat
before encountering Truth.
What moves him to pray
if not the glimpse of the Just One's grace within prayer?

77

My role is that of a soldier, and of selflessness;
my Sovereign's role is to grant life.
Blessed is the head upheld by the king hand;
unfortunate is the head that bows to another.

78

They exist for God, not for wealth;
they die for God, not out of fear or anguish.

79

We are unconcerned with the acceptability of our deeds;
our duty is to submit and comply with the directive.
He has imposed this enslavement upon us;
we possess no autonomy over ourselves in this matter.

80

In addition to surrender and acceptance,
what other solution exists?
In the lion's paw, you are but a blood-filled beast.
He knows neither rest nor nourishment, like the sun;
He liberates souls from slumber and deprivation.
'Join Me, or emulate Me,
so that you may perceive the revelation of My appearance.'

Part 9

The Responsibilities of Humanity on the Path of Spiritual Journey

81

For seven centuries, the path has existed
where he resolved to embark on a quest for love.
He yearned for the physical journey,
yet his spirit ascended to the highest realms.
The valiant horsemen forged ahead in their pursuits,
while the imprudent lay waiting in ambush.

82

General compliance is a transgression for the elite;
universal conformity veils the unique and particular.

83

When they are uncertain of the path,
they drift aimlessly, following the crowd.
They rely on faith as a blacksmith on his forge.
What purpose does their battle serve?
Trust is similarly tossed about like dice.

84

Even so, with this expression, rise higher;
for the domain of God is vast and welcoming.
This intoxication resembles a white bird
soaring above sacred ground.

85

No affliction is greater than the delusion of perfection;
it exists not within you,
O one of charm.
From your heart and eyes,
blood may seep
until this self-adulation is relinquished.

86

Return to the mine like gold,
so that your hands may be liberated from impurities.

87

The wolf often attacks
when a lamb wanders away from the herd.
He who forsakes the community's path,
who will not shed their own blood?
Tradition serves as the route;
the community acts as a companion.
Without guidance and companionship,
you may encounter difficulties.

88

In any circumstance, you continually seek,
perpetually yearning for water,
O parched lips.

89

Abraham avoided destruction and carried on;
he renounced glory and left.
This one is unscathed, and this one is burnt.
How strange! It is the inverse horseshoe during
the journey of exploration.

90

A solitary particle in the shade of grace
surpasses many endeavours in devoted dedication.

Part 10
Responsibility Towards Thoughts & Inner States

91

As the embodiment of the exquisite bride emerges,
isolation accompanies this station with her.
The monarch perceives the manifestation, as do others;
yet, once on his own, it is for the cherished king alone.

92

The curse of perception lies in its habitual nature; cleaning blood with blood is both impossible and nonsensical.

93

Seal your lips, even if eloquence has favoured you;
do not speak,
for God possesses the ultimate
understanding of instruction.
O perpetually intoxicated one,
perched on the edge of a rooftop,
maintain humility, or fall.
Peace be with you.

94

An image must originate from cherished companions,
enabling you to extract water from
the ocean of formlessness.
An image is merely an imitation;
its repetition reveals the truth.

95

The murmurs of disclosure and recommendation
originate from many,
not a single source.

96

A fresh desire for You emerges
in the hallowed mosque of Your essence.
You, like Solomon, administer justice;
emulate Him,
yet do not infringe upon Him.

97

A person has numerous concealed enemies;
the wise exercise prudence and discernment.
Ordinary people, with their concealed flaws and strengths,
incessantly assail the heart.

98

This body acts as a guesthouse:
each morning, a new guest arrives in haste.
Do not say:
'This has weighed around my neck.'
For whatever it is can abruptly dissolve into oblivion.
Embrace whatever emerges from the invisible realm,
for it is a visitor to be treasured in your heart.

99

Any uplifting call originates from a higher source.
Any appeal that provokes your greed,
acknowledge it as the lament of a wolf
inflicting suffering upon humanity.

100

Silence now, that the king may address us.
Do not barter this blossom with your melody.
This flower is expressive, vibrant, and strong.
O nightingale,
be silent and rejoice.

Finis

www.ingramcontent.com/pod-product-compliance
Lightning Source LLC
Chambersburg PA
CBHW020451100426
42813CB00031B/3323/J